THE
Future
Architect's
TOOL KIT

Barbara Beck
ARCHITECT

THE
Future
Architect's
TOOL KIT

Barbara Beck
ARCHITECT

Schiffer Publishing Ltd®

4880 Lower Valley Road • Atglen, PA 19310

Other Schiffer Books by Barbara Beck:

The Future Architect's Handbook, ISBN 978-0-7643-4676-7

Other Schiffer Books on Related Subjects:

Christopher Wren: Avian Architect, Tina Skinner, ISBN 978-0-7643-3169-5

Saltbox House: Color 'n Build Activity Playset, ISBN 978-0-7643-3443-6

Library of Congress Control Number: 2016943737

Designed by Justin Watkinson
Type set in ITC American Typewriter/ConduitOSITC

ISBN: 978-0-7643-5193-8
Printed in China

Published by Schiffer Publishing, Ltd.
4880 Lower Valley Road
Atglen, PA 19310
Phone: (610) 593-1777; Fax: (610) 593-2002
E-mail: Info@schifferbooks.com
Web: www.schifferbooks.com

For our complete selection of fine books on this and related subjects, please visit our website at www.schifferbooks.com. You may also write for a free catalog.

Schiffer Publishing's titles are available at special discounts for bulk purchases for sales promotions or premiums. Special editions, including personalized covers, corporate imprints, and excerpts, can be created in large quantities for special needs. For more information, contact the publisher.

We are always looking for people to write books on new and related subjects. If you have an idea for a book, please contact us at proposals@schifferbooks.com.

CONTENTS

ACKNOWLEDGMENTS

Thanks to my husband, Richard Compton; to fellow architect and friend Jean Johnson Rose; and to Aaron Novack, the inspiration for Aaron the Architect!

Buildings are where we work, play, and go to school.
Buildings shelter us from the weather.
Buildings provide places to live.

Architecture is the art and science of building. The art of architecture means a building captivates our senses and is pleasing to see. The science of architecture is how a building is physically constructed.

A person who is trained in architecture and passes a licensing exam is an architect. The word architect comes from the Greek word *architektón,* which means master builder, but an architect is not a builder. An architect decides how a building should look, how it should work, and how it should fit within its surroundings. He or she then creates drawings that are used as patterns for construction.

In *The Future Architect's Handbook,* you studied the drawings for Aaron the Architect's house. In *The Future Architect's Tool Kit,* you will create drawings for your own house. You will also meet a few clients who want you to design for them.

This workbook includes an architecture tool kit like the one Aaron used. It will help you draw any building you can imagine.

The appendix contains building elements that you can trace and insert in your own drawings. There is also a pattern to build a model of Aaron's house.

Now let's design!

CHAPTER ONE

A Short Review

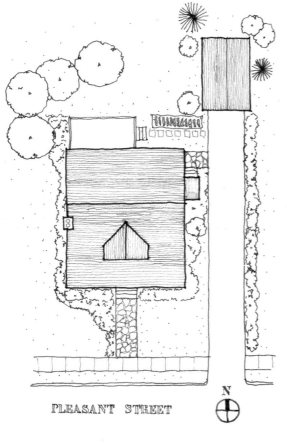

PLEASANT STREET

N

SITE PLAN

FLOOR PLAN

DECK

DINING ROOM

KITCHEN

BATH

LIVING ROOM

BEDROOM

PORCH

Every architect everywhere in the world creates drawings that are used as patterns for construction. These drawings are the *Site Plan*, *Floor Plan*, *Section*, and *Elevation*.

SECTION B

ELEVATION

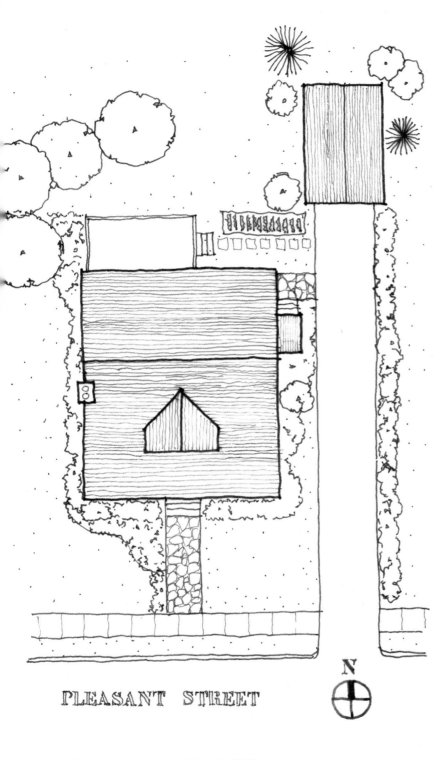

PLEASANT STREET

N

SITE PLAN

The site is the land on which a building sits and the nearby surroundings. The Site Plan is what a bird sees from the air.

A bird flying over Aaron's property would see the roofs of his house and garage. Swooping lower, the bird would see Aaron's back deck, his vegetable garden, and the street on which he lives. The bird might see Aaron's dog, Artemis, standing in his front yard, but Artemis doesn't appear on Aaron's Site Plan. Only things physically attached to his property are shown on the Site Plan.

Like the Site Plan, the Floor Plan is an overhead view. It is the view we see if we slice the walls of a house parallel to the ground, attach a crane to the upper part of the building, lift it off, and then fly over in a plane and look down.

One major difference between the Site Plan and the Floor Plan is the size of the house on the drawing. The Site Plan shows the overall layout of the property, including the house, but the house is not the main focus. On the other hand, the Floor Plan drawing looks specifically at the house and the placement of its rooms and doors and windows, and not the landscape surrounding it. The Floor Plan's larger size helps us see those details.

A house might have one Floor Plan. It might have ten! It all depends on how many levels the house has.

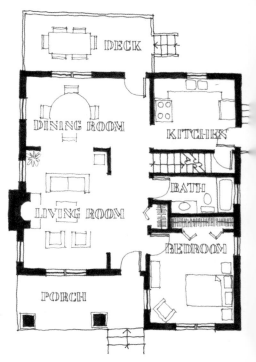

FLOOR PLAN

BASEMENT PLAN   **FLOOR PLAN**   **ATTIC PLAN**

Floor plans are a lot like a deck of cards. Aaron's house has a basement, a main floor, and an attic. The Basement Plan is like the bottom card. His First Floor Plan is above that, and topping the deck is the Attic Plan.

Aaron's Site Plan shows what the roof of his house looks like. If it had shown only the outline of his house, he would need a separate Roof Plan.

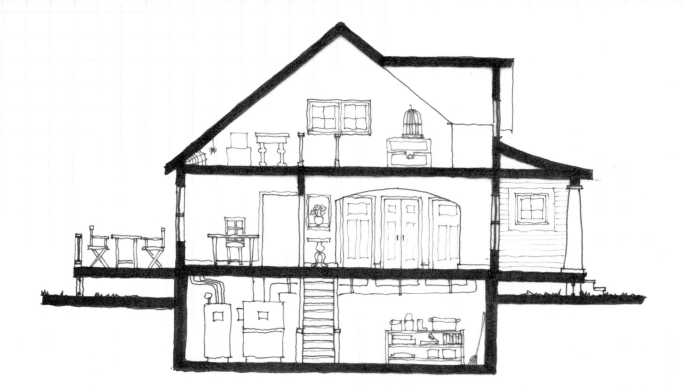

SECTION B

While the Floor Plan is a view looking down, the Section slices the building vertically from roof to ground. We see what is happening on all floor levels simultaneously, similar to the way we look at a dollhouse.

The Section helps us understand what a building looks like on the inside, how tall it should be, and how it is constructed.

Once we know how our house works on the inside, we can decide how it looks from the outside. Drawing an *Elevation* helps.

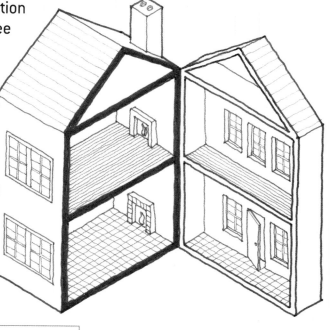

SOUTH ELEVATION

The front of a building is sometimes called its façade. *Façade* sounds like *face*. Like a painter might draw a portrait of your face, an architect draws a portrait of the house's face—the Elevation! You can't change the location of your nose and mouth and eyes, but using an Elevation, an architect can rearrange the features of the building's face to make them appeal to the eye.

There are usually four elevations, identified by the direction they face—North, South, East, and West. Elevations can also be labeled Front, Back, and Side. The front elevation of Aaron's house faces south, so it might be called the Front (South) Elevation.

If the side of a building faces some special environmental feature, like the ocean, that view might be called the Oceanfront Elevation. Whatever you call your elevation, be specific!

CHAPTER TWO

The Design Kit

Once upon a time, architects prepared drawings by hand.

They used pencils, pens, erasers, *lots* of paper, and probably the architect's most famous drafting tool, a T-square. Not surprisingly, the T-square earned its name because it looks like the letter T!

The T-square helped architects draw straight horizontal lines. Another tool, the triangle, placed along one edge of the T-square, helped an architect draw vertical lines. Can you find the T-square and triangle in the drawing above?

Today, most architects draw on the computer. A computer takes up less space than a drafting table, the drawings are clean (no messy pencil smudges), green (no piles of paper to throw away), and the only equipment needed is a computer.

Like other architects, Aaron uses a computer. He also likes to draw by hand. If he wants to draw straight lines without a T-square or triangle, he uses special paper.

Your design kit includes a pencil and eraser. It also includes a tablet of Aaron's special paper, called graph paper. A grid superimposed on each sheet will help you draw straight lines, but more importantly, the paper will help you draw to scale.

You remember scale, don't you? Scale is a system of measurement. It is how the size of a drawn object compares to its actual size. Scale enables an architect to draw a huge building a fraction of its real size so that it fits onto a sheet of paper.

The small squares on your graph paper measure ¼" in each direction, representing 1 foot of length in the real world. In other words, the scale of this paper is ¼" = 1'. Most residential floor plans are drawn at this scale. You can use graph paper for section and elevation drawings, too. See how special it is!

What if you want to draw a building and you don't have graph paper? You can create drawings on any paper using another famous architectural tool, the *scale.*

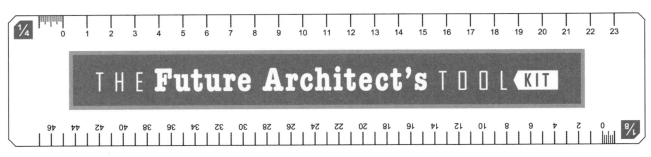

The two-sided architect's scale included in your design kit provides four different scales, two on each side: ⅛", ¼", ½", and 1'.

The house shown on Aaron's Site Plan is a different size from the one on his Floor Plan because he used different scales. Aaron drew his Floor Plan at ¼" scale. But, in order to show everything on his property and fit the drawing on the same size paper as the Floor Plan, he used a smaller scale for his Site Plan.

Remember, the larger the scale, the smaller the area you see. On the other hand, the smaller the scale, the wider the view.

Now that you are acquainted with your design kit, let's design.

CHAPTER THREE

Let's Design

Design is problem solving and creativity mixed together. It is both process and desired outcome. The outcome we want is a house. Maybe the house looks like Aaron's. Maybe it's totally different. That decision is part of the design process.

In *The Future Architect's Handbook*, you learned that an important aspect of the design process involves respect for the physical features of the property—the topography, vegetation, climate, and orientation of the elements on the site.

During winter, trees lose their leaves and let warming sunshine into south-facing rooms. Trees also shelter buildings from cold north winds. They provide nesting places for birds.

If the property is hilly, situating a building atop the hill might give it a wonderful view, help catch summer breezes, or give it a feeling of importance.

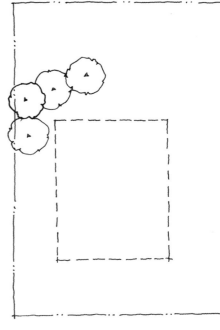

Placing a building in a valley protects it from winter winds.

These factors influence how we live inside the house. They also affect our mood.

Another aspect of the design process includes working within certain rules. While we would like to build whatever we wish, it isn't always possible. Most cities have building codes, which are rules limiting what can and cannot be built. The rules apply to houses as well as skyscrapers.

In Aaron's neighborhood, the building code limited how close to his property line he could build his house. That distance is called a *setback.* On the drawing at top right, the outer dashed lines represent Aaron's property line. The inner dashed lines are where he was allowed to build because of the city's setbacks.

You can see how the building code influenced Aaron's final Site Plan.

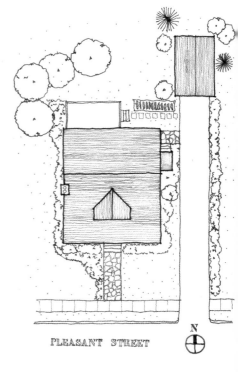

PLEASANT STREET

N

SITE PLAN

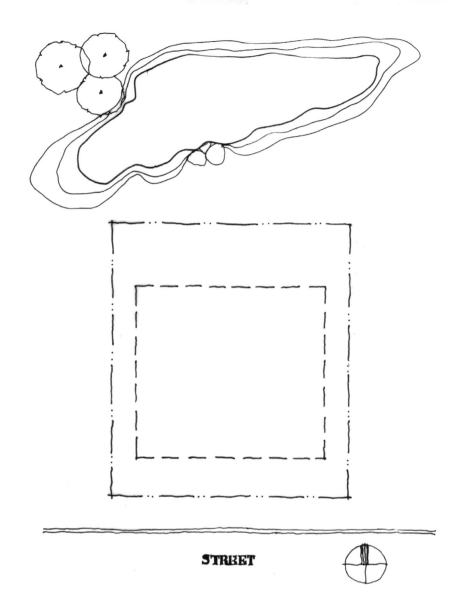

STREET

It's time to start your design! We'll work through the process, step-by-step.

Assume you have a piece of property shaped like a rectangle. The land is almost flat, with only a gentle slope downhill to the north. The north and south sides are 30 feet long, while the east and west sides are each 35 feet in length. A quiet street borders the south side of your lot. People often walk past your property on their way to nearby shops. Neighboring houses are on the east and west, and are two-story dwellings. The climate has hot summers and cold winters. Large maple trees on your property overlook a park that has a lake where children sail model boats.

Using the description and the previous illustration to guide you, draw the outline of your property on a piece of graph paper from your tool kit. Remember, each small square represents 1 foot of length in the real world.

Here's a hint to help you get started: The north side of your property should face the top of the page. That's easy to remember if you think about a map of the world. The North Pole is located at the top. To avoid confusion, however, always draw an arrow pointing north.

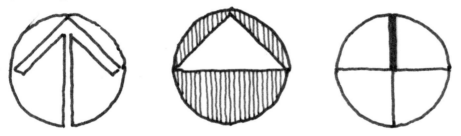

The building code says your house must fit within a boundary 5 feet from the street, 8 feet from the rear (north) property line, and 3 feet from each side. The setbacks form the outline of your house, also called its *footprint.* Just as your foot creates a mark on the earth, so does a building.

You have now located the outside, or exterior, walls of your house.

Stand in the open doorway of any building and look sideways at the wall. Notice its thickness. The wall is an important building component. It not only encloses and protects the inside of the building, it also acts as *structure to support the house.*

Do you remember structure? Structure is like a person's skeleton. It holds the building upright against gravity, high winds, and even earthquakes.

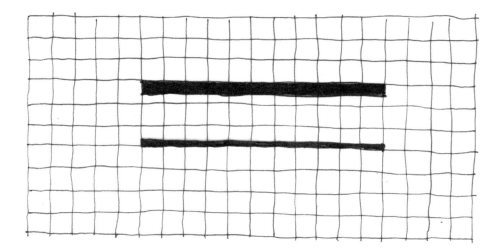

Walls are made of wood and steel and concrete, so the walls you draw must represent those materials. A 6"-thick line is a good approximation of an exterior wall. Interior walls are drawn thinner (3" thick) because they are constructed of fewer layers. The drawing above shows what a 6" wall and a 3" wall look like in plan.

Let's move inside your house and work on the Floor Plan. If you are confused about how to draw something, look in the appendix. It contains standard architectural symbols.

Starting a new design can be a little scary, or maybe you just don't know how to begin. Architects sometimes feel the same, so they often use a *bubble diagram* to help them get started.

In a bubble diagram, each bubble, or circle, represents a room. The size of a bubble indicates its importance—the larger the bubble, the more important it is.

A bubble can represent things other than rooms. For instance, it might represent a beautiful view or an idea, such as, "I want to use solar power," or "I like castles," or even "My bedroom must be orange!" The arrangement of the bubbles helps determine where rooms should be located. Bubble diagrams often turn into floor plans.

SUNLIGHT

DECK

GARDEN

COOK

FIREPLACE

LIVING

BATH   CLOSET

EATING

SLEEP

CLOSET

ENTRY

Think about what you want in your house. You probably need a place to cook, a place to eat, and a place to sleep. You may need spaces for other activities, too.

Do you play games?

Dance?

Your interests determine the size and arrangement of rooms in your house.

Maybe you need only one room in your house. Maybe you need lots of rooms. Think about how and where you want to enter the house, then imagine going the other way, from inside to out. Think about sunlight and views—the park and your neighbors, big windows versus small ones. Think about the house you live in. What do you like about it? What do you dislike? Certain rooms are standard sizes. Most hallways are 3 feet wide. Most doors, too. In general, living rooms are larger than bedrooms, and bedrooms are larger than bathrooms, but they don't have to be!

People have different reactions to different size spaces. Imagine being inside a closet, which is small and dark. Compare that feeling to what it would be like inside a Gothic cathedral with its lofty ceilings and stained-glass windows.

The amount of light coming into a room affects how people feel, so don't forget to locate doors and windows on your Floor Plan! Their locations will also help you see how much wall space is available for art or furniture or structural support.

If you are designing a two-story house, you need a staircase or an elevator (or both!) to link the levels of the house. A staircase also links the floor plans, so it needs to be in the same relative position on each drawing. Think of a stair as a vertical hallway. Like a hallway, a staircase is usually 3 feet wide. Here are some common staircases *in plan.*

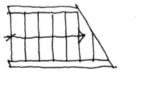
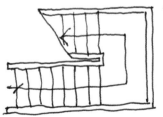

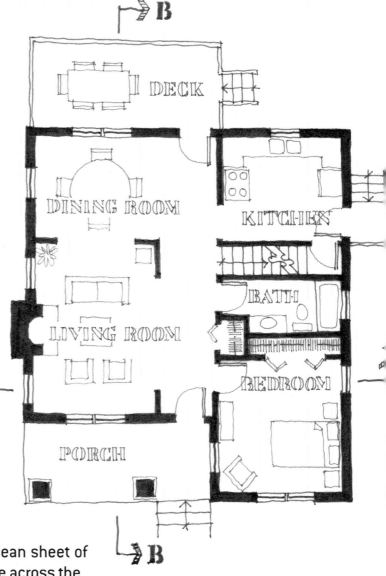

When you are satisfied with your Floor Plan, start the Section. You don't have to have a perfect floor plan at this point. In fact, it can be helpful to work on both drawings simultaneously.

Draw a line down the middle of your floor plan to show where you are slicing the building into two sections. Decide in which direction you want to look, and then draw arrows on the plan to show which way you are facing. Label the sections A or B if you are creating more than one section. Your drawing might look something like this.

Place your Floor Plan drawing next to a clean sheet of paper. On the new sheet, draw a horizontal line across the page using the grid as a guide. That line represents a floor.

FLOOR PLAN

Like walls, floors are part of a building's structure. They are constructed of beams and joists and floorboards. Assume your floor structure is 12 inches deep. Draw a line parallel to the first one 12 inches below it. You floor is complete. Now draw a 6"-thick vertical line at one end of your floor. Measure the width of your house and draw a second vertical line that distance from the first. Those are your exterior walls.

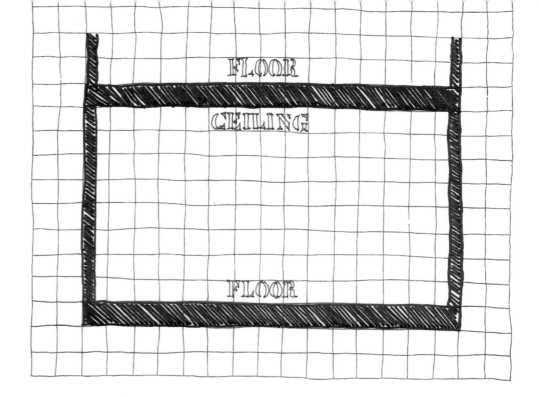

Most houses have 8' ceilings, but some are taller. Scale up 8' from the floor and draw another 12"-thick line. This represents the ceiling of one story and the floor of the level above. Your drawing will look something like this.

What if you had drawn the ceiling 10' high? Would you feel different in that room? What if the ceiling were 6' high?

You have now drawn two floors—the basement and first floor, or the first and second floor. If your house has multiple stories, repeat the process.

Notice how the ceiling height establishes the overall building height. Building codes often restrict the height of houses, but your building code allows a house to be as high or as deep into the earth as you want. And remember, buildings don't float in space, so always draw the earth as a big fat line holding up your house!

What kind of roof do you envision on your house? A gable? Hip? Mansard?

This is what each roof mentioned above looks like in Section.

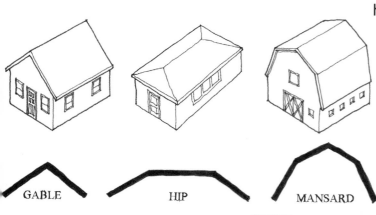

GABLE HIP MANSARD

SECTION   B

At this point, you have completed the Section. Does it look like Aaron's or is it completely different?

Overlay another piece of paper on top of the section and draw the outline of the house. The outline of the Section is the also the outline for the Elevation!

Draw the doors and windows where you located them on your plan. You can always change their locations if you don't like the way everything looks together. Architects do that all the time. Just make sure the locations on the plans and elevations match when you are finished.

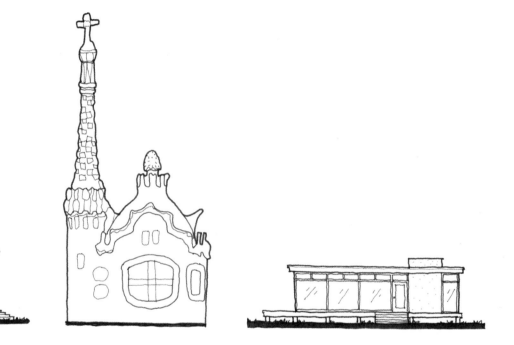

Many houses today look like buildings from the past.

See how the doors and windows vary with each style. The neo-classical house on the left looks a lot like Greek architecture. The modern house has large windows and stresses horizontal elements. Use one of these or make up your own style. There are no wrong designs.

CHAPTER FOUR

Building a Model

In *The Future Architect's Handbook*, Aaron the Architect hired a construction crew to build his house. They dug the hole for the basement, poured the concrete foundation walls, and built the house on top of that.

Even before construction began, Aaron wanted to see what his house would look like in three dimensions, so he built a model. You can use his technique to make a model of your design.

You need your scale, scissors, tape or glue, thin cardboard for the walls and roof, and a thick piece of cardboard as a base for the model. A cardboard box is a good source for material.

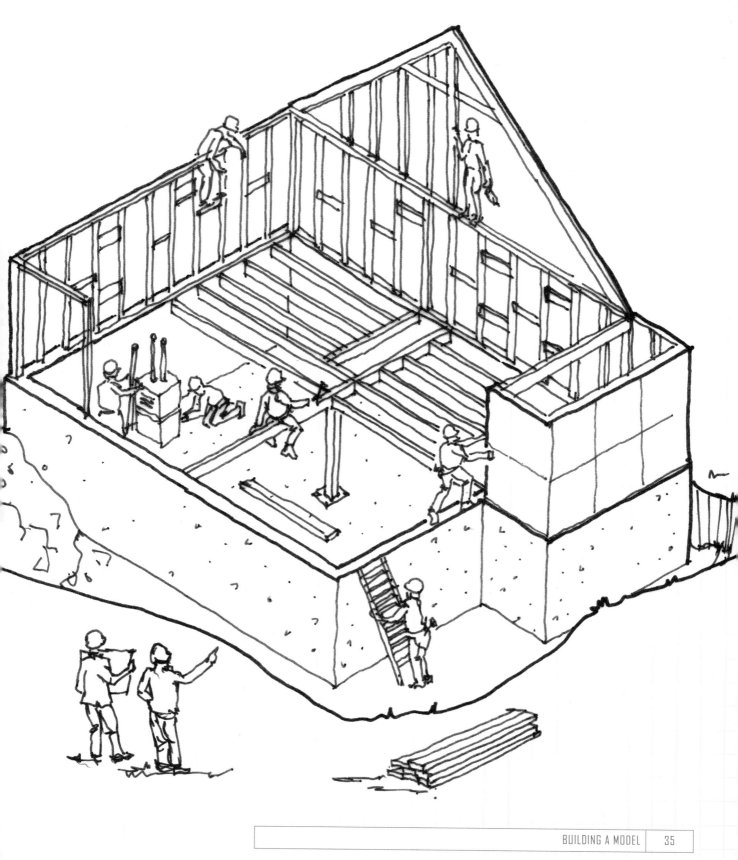

You can use an X-acto knife instead of scissors to cut out your model, but then you will need a metal ruler as a guide to cut straight lines. Don't use an X-acto with a wooden ruler because the blade might slip over the edge and cut you! And never use your scale as a cutting guide or you might ruin it. You will also need a cutting board so your parents don't get mad at you for slicing up their favorite antique! Make sure you cut in a direction away from your fingers.

Before you start, trace your floor plan and elevations onto another sheet of paper, or scan and print a copy of each one. That way you will have a copy of your design and won't have to start from scratch if you want to re-design the house.

STEP ONE: Cut out the floor plan. Leave a small border outside of the walls.

STEP TWO: Tape or glue your floor plan onto the cardboard base. You will erect your walls on the outline of your house, just like in real construction.

STEP THREE: Tape or glue your elevations onto a piece of the thin cardboard. You have several choices at this point. You can make the walls one continual piece, like in the drawing above. This is how Aaron built his model. The pattern for his house is in the appendix.

Cut around the outline of the elevation with scissors or an X-acto knife. After that, score where each wall joins the next, which basically means to lightly cut the walls so that the cardboard is easy to fold. If you accidentally cut all the way through the cardboard, don't worry. You can still build your model, because another option is to cut out each wall separately. Draw a 1" border along the side of each wall. That border becomes a surface that the adjacent walls can be glued to. If your wall has already been cut out, attach a 1" tab to each side and you are ready to glue the walls together.

STEP FOUR: Attach the walls to the base.

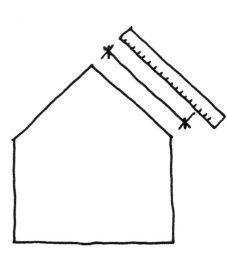

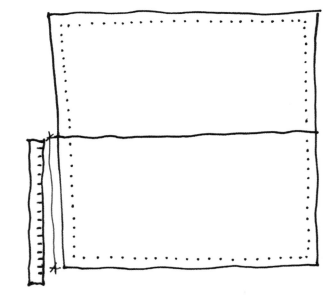

STEP FIVE: Before you cut out the roof, go outside and look at the roof of your house. It extends beyond the walls. This overhang helps the roof shed rain and snow. Your model roof also needs an overhang. It won't keep water out of your model, but it will help you attach the roof to the house.

Let's say you have a gabled roof like Aaron's house. The actual roof is larger than it appears in plan because the plan looks straight down, while the roof is angled like the side of a triangle. You need to measure the actual length.

Measure one angled side of the roof. Mark your cardboard with that dimension, remembering to add an extra 6" for the overhang.

Next, measure the length of the roof and mark the distance. This corresponds to one side of the roof. Repeat for the other side.

Cut out the roof and glue to the walls.

Your model is almost complete! Draw the location of trees and sidewalks on your cardboard base to show how your house fits within its environment. What do you think?

You don't need cardboard to build a model. Collect bags of recycled materials such as cans, plastic water bottles, paper, string, foil, and egg cartons. Create a model using those. Don't be limited by anything. Use your imagination!

CHAPTER FIVE

Meet Your Clients!

Most buildings would never be built without *clients.* Clients hire architects to create buildings especially suited for their needs. A client can be one person, like the owner of a house, or a group of people. Schools, libraries, and churches are examples of buildings with more than one client. The client determines who occupies the building and how the building is used. In fact, the client helps shape what a building looks like almost as much as the architect!

You are now a famous architect! The individuals listed at the end of this chapter all want you to work for them.

Using your architect's kit and the skills you learned here and in *The Future Architect's Handbook*, design something for each client that meets his or her unique requirements. Start with a bubble diagram and then move on to the floor plan. Once you are satisfied, draw sections and elevations. You can even build a model.

To remind yourself that what you are designing is for your client, draw a picture of your client if there isn't one shown. Keep the picture nearby as you design. It will help you create something that will make your client happy. A happy client makes a happy architect.

List the things your client needs—a sleeping area, an entertaining area, an eating area. Go beyond that. Think about who your client is and what he or she likes to do—paint, cook, play. What can you design to fulfill those needs? If your client loves flowers, maybe you can propose big windows overlooking a garden. If your client loves water, a swimming pool or giant bathtub might be perfect.

Don't worry about building codes. There are no rules where your clients live!

It's time to meet your clients. He-ere they are!

A **kindly giant** who thinks he is a hobbit

A **dolphin** who likes to watch TV

A **vegetarian crocodile** who loves to cook

An **astronaut** who refuses to take off his space suit, angering his wife

A **wheelchair-bound dog** who plays soccer

A **swimmer** who wants a portable changing room to take to the beach

A **father, mother, and their twelve children** who travel the country as musicians

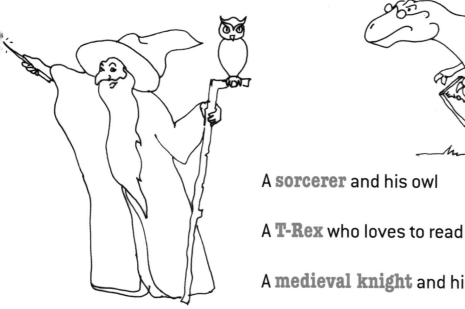

A **sorcerer** and his owl

A **T-Rex** who loves to read

A **medieval knight** and his horse

The **medieval knight's page** who has to shine the knight's armor every day

An **eccentric millionaire** who wants to live inside an amusement park

An **Eskimo** who loves igloos, but hates winter and is moving to Florida

Who else could use your design expertise? Your parents? Your friends? Your pet?

Create a portfolio of your work—a place to keep sketches, tracings, and magazine clippings. Your portfolio can be something as simple as a manila folder or as complex as you want. Not only is it fun to look at old designs, it helps you create new ones.

Remember, design is problem solving and creativity mixed together. Good architecture applies to a house, a neighborhood, a city, and even a nation.

Now go out there and design!

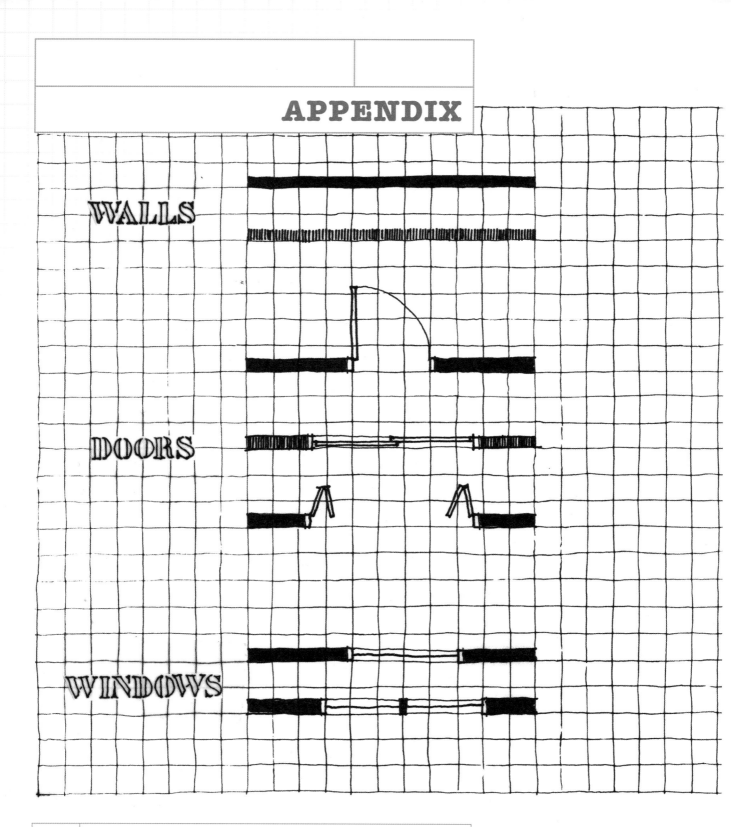

APPENDIX

WALLS

DOORS

WINDOWS

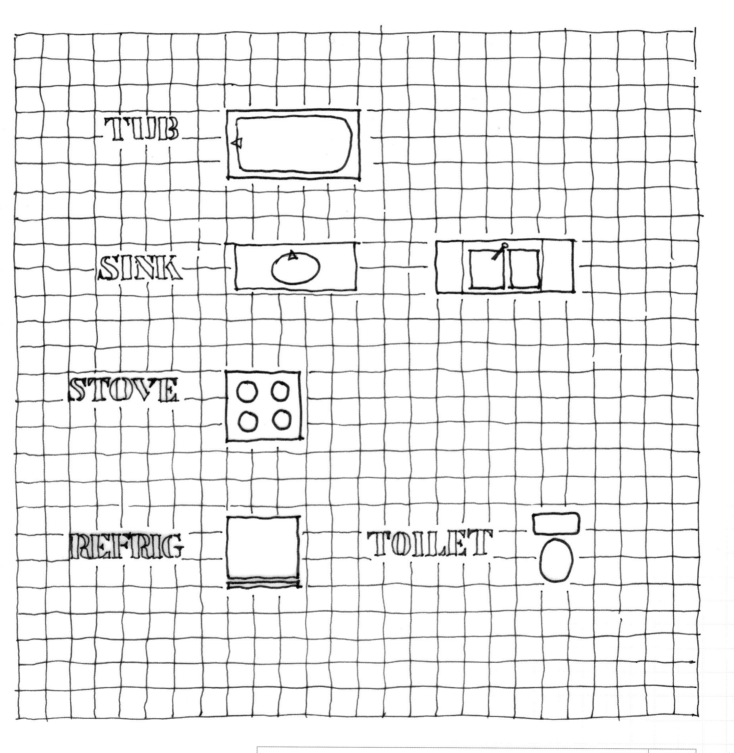

TUB

SINK

STOVE

REFRIG

TOILET

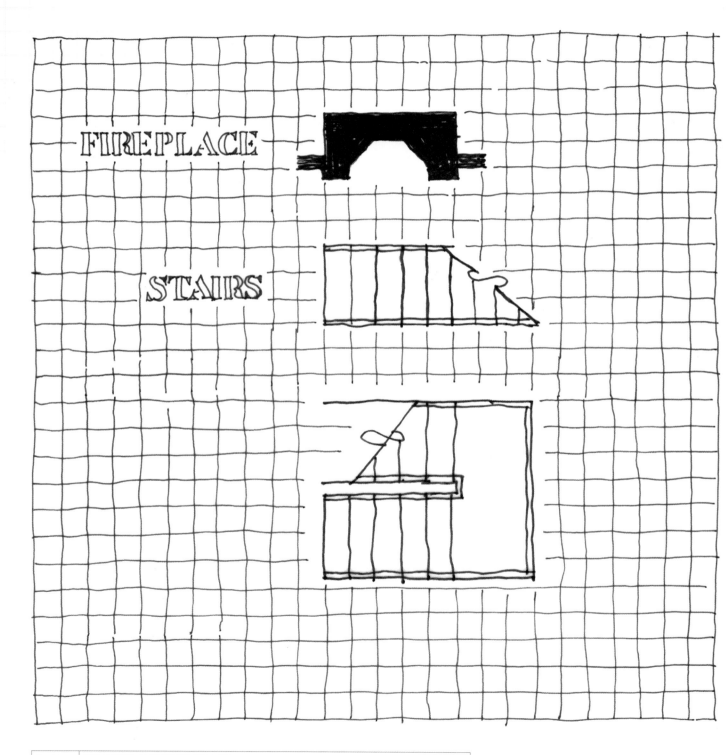

FIREPLACE

STAIRS

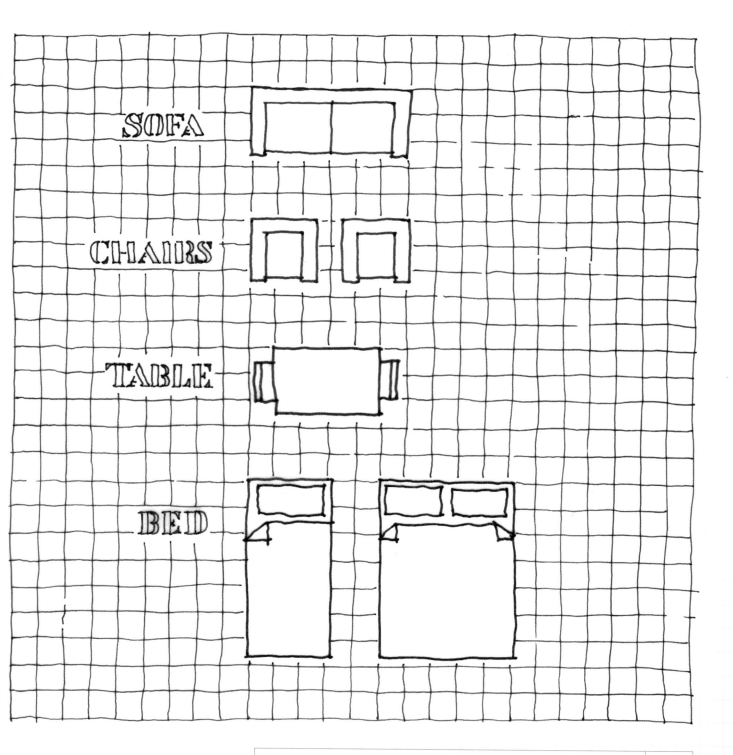

SOFA

CHAIRS

TABLE

BED

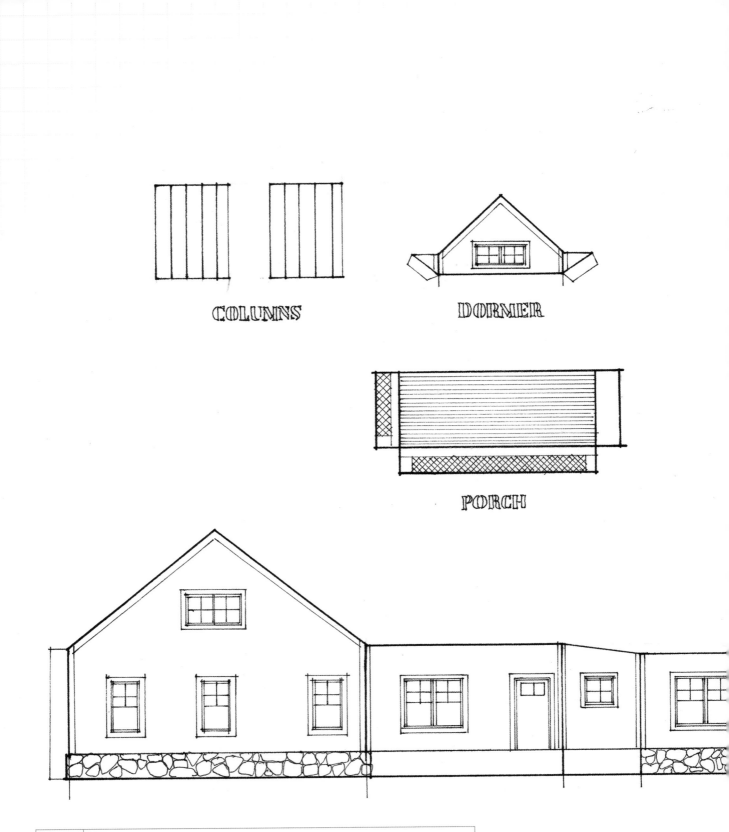

COLUMNS

DORMER

PORCH

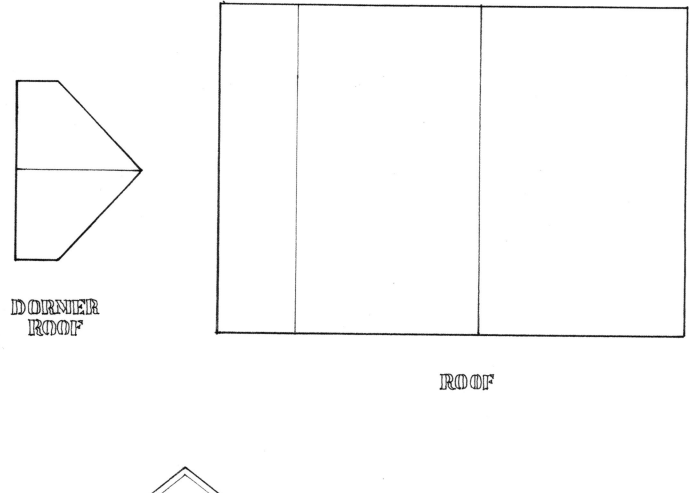

DORNER ROOF

ROOF

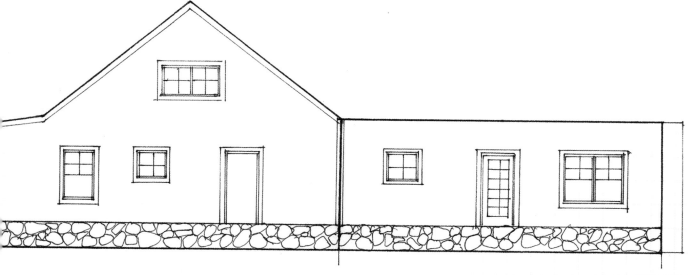

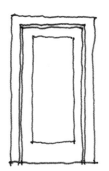

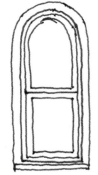